DOG FARTS

Written By:
Herbert Kavet

Illustrated By:
Martin Riskin

Manufactured in the United States of America

30 29 28 27 26 25 24 23 22 21 20 19 18 17 16 15 14 13 12 11 10 9 8 7 6 5 4 3 2 1

Ivory Tower Publishing Co., Inc.
125 Walnut St., P.O. Box 9132, Watertown, MA 02272-9132
Telephone #: (617) 923-1111   Fax #: (617) 923-8839

INTRODUCTION

It's not too important what I write here. The kind of people buying a book on dog farts aren't going to waste their time reading "Introductions," but are probably going to dive right into the meat of the subject. To insure that the few intellectuals at the Library of Congress who might check up on details are satisfied, I'll use this space to thank my dog, Kelev, for all the insight he gave me on this subject during those winter, closed window, three hour rides up to Vermont.

HOW THIS BOOK WAS WRITTEN

The research for this book was carried out in the living rooms, cars and kitchens of friends and relatives. People were interviewed, some of whom refused to acknowledge that their dogs fart and others who would toss their pets out of the house at the first sign of an emission. Big dogs whose farts caused rooms full of guests' eyes to water were examined as well as innocent canines whose owner blamed their own farts on the animal.

It's not a glamourous subject, but as they say, someone has to do it and as long as that someone is me, I might as well add a few cartoons by the brilliant dog farting cartoonist, Marty Riskin, and make a few bucks selling this twaddle. No one ever went broke underestimating the taste of the American public.

CLASSIFYING DOG FARTS

Most dog farts seem to come out of a reclining animal. Relaxed and content, the fart slips out quietly while your dog is lying there harboring a look of total innocence. Were it not for the God-awful smell, you'd continue to think all was well in the world.

This book will classify dog farts by foods, breed and whatever else I can think of, 'cause it's not easy to come up with a whole book of dog farts, believe me.

CLASSIFYING DOG FARTS

The majority of dog farts are silent farts. Noisy farts usually require a conscious act on the part of the farter and dogs are generally too unconcerned about farts to make this effort. When enough pressure builds up to punch a fart out, it will just happen. The dog's not going to do a damn thing to help it along.

THE GRASS FART

No one knows why dogs sometimes eat grass. Perhaps it is to get some vitamins lacking in their diet, but more likely because dogs always seem to be hungry, and often times, it's the only stuff around. Dogs' stomachs just aren't designed to digest grass and it'll make them fart, sure as shooting. The lucky thing is grass farts seldom have an offensive odor and most people hardly notice they have occurred.

THE LEFTOVER TURKEY FART

This fart is common about six days after Thanksgiving. The palatability of the leftover turkey on the lower shelf of the refrigerator is getting a little questionable and, in one form or another, ends up in Fido's bowl. I guess dogs just aren't supposed to eat turkey, because the leftover turkey produces some of the worst odors of any dog fart. You'll be happy the relatives have all gone home when this fart fills your living room, and if they haven't left yet, they soon will.

THE CAT FOOD FART

Homes that keep both cats and dogs as pets are asking for trouble. A finicky cat often is unconcerned about its food and leaves it in the bowl for hours or longer. Old Rover, of course, has no such qualms and will gobble it down, should the opportunity arise. The resulting Cat Food Fart is horrendous in its intensity, and the fish or liver base of the cat food gives this fart a staying power that is truly awesome. Plan on leaving your house for two or three days if the fart occurs indoors.

THE INNOCENT DOG FART

Most dogs have the ability to put on the most innocent expression as soon as they have farted. Their master may call out their name in an angry voice but old "Prince" just cocks his head, as if to ask what the trouble is all about. Even dog psychiatrists have been unable to discover if this is just an act or pure naivete.

THE STRAINING ON A LEASH FART

Here we have an unusual standing up fart and, what is even rarer, a standing fart that is frequently audible. Your powerful pet is straining to get an innocent squirrel or perhaps another dog. All his or her muscles are strained and pulling, and lo and behold, out comes a big one. Fortunately, this fart usually occurs in the great outdoors so it is seldom terribly offensive.

THE CHLOROPHYLL FART

Remember when chlorophyll was all the rage and chlorophyll pills and additives were supposed to make everyone's breath smell sweet? Did you ever believe the stuff worked? Well you might not believe the check is in the mail or in the existence of the tooth fairy but you'd better believe that eating grass is mother nature's way of insuring the dogs get some chlorophyll so at least some dog farts are acceptable in polite company.

THE TV FART

Probably the most common dog fart there is. Either lying at your feet while watching TV triggers something in a dog to make it fart, or people just spend so much time in front of the TV that most farts simply occur here. Whatever its cause, the TV Fart elicits only minimum response from the family—usually a groan on the order of "Ohhh, Boy" and seldom as stern as "Out, Boy! Out!"

THE TV FART

If you'd really like to discover the truth behind TV Farts, you could, I suppose, buy a video we recently produced called "A Video For Your Dog" (only $9.95). This video entertains dogs with everything from fire hydrants to mailmen with lots of barking, bones and little animals to keep your pet's interest. Put this twenty minute video into your VCR, plop your dog down and then hide behind the curtain to see what happens. Write and tell me. I'd like to know, too.

THE BAD BREATH FART

This, of course, isn't a fart at all but bad breath. A dog's breath can be so bad that you'd wish it were a fart, which is where this name came from. Hey, look at all the places the tongue has been during the day. More accidents have been caused by pets leaning over the car seat and breathing in the driver's face than all the speeding and drinkers you read about.

THE HORSE MANURE FART

Those of you who keep horses know this terrible secret. Horses produce copious quantities of manure and dogs find the stuff irresistible, if you get my drift. The resulting farts are of a double whammy nature and you better hope they are let loose in the barn rather than in your living room.

THE WELCOME FART

The full name of this fart is the Jump Up And Lick Your Face When You Come Home Welcome Fart. Since dogs don't usually have much of a concept of time, this fart can occur every time they see you even, for example, if you've just gone to the garage for a rake. Anyhow, this is an excited can't-hold-it in fart which wouldn't be so annoying but for the fact your loving beast is farting all over you as she or he licks your face.

THE GUILTY DOG FART

Every now and then a dog that has been condemned over the years for many intestinal transgressions and censured in no uncertain terms for each fart, will cut a big one and immediately assume a guilty posture. This is exactly the attitude you'd expect in a well-trained dog, and the look of contrition makes the offense much more bearable.

THE GROOMING FART

There you are, brushing and loving your pooch, perhaps stroking a little too firmly, and you squeeze out a fart and you say, "Oooh, Scotty." But Scotty knows you caused it and can't be less concerned. You're probably grinning a little in embarrassment, as well.

THE FRENCH FRIES FART

Here's how it happens. Some kid spills his french fries in the parking lot at McDonald's, and Duke is out stretching his paws after a long car trip and isn't about to pass up some free grub. The farting begins after the family is back in the car.

THE CHOKE CHAIN FART

Professional dog trainers rely on the choke chain as a highly effective training device. Soft-hearted dog owners, however, have traditionally been reluctant to use them. As it turns out, this choke chain is the single largest cause of dog farting there is. Think of your dog, if you will, as a sausage with two openings. A choke chain cuts off the top one, leaving only the nether for whatever pressure imbalance the dog's system develops. You'll notice that dog trainers almost always work outdoors.

THE CANDY FART

This is a seasonal fart, most common around Halloween. The kids come home with a big bag of candy, which lies around their room until the poor pet just can't withstand the temptation. Once started, the whole bag of candy is savaged, probably until doggy throws up. The farts come a bit later and will make your children swear off chocolate for a month.

THE IN HEAT FART

When dogs are thinking about sex, they never lie down and relax long enough to fart. There is no such thing as an "In Heat Fart" and anyone who says there is makes a mockery of this whole dog fart classification business.

THE PICK-UP TRUCK FART

Hey, who cares? The hound is in the back and can fart his or her brains out without disturbing people, so why bother? This fart would be totally unknown were it not for an occasional hitchhiker who sits in back.

THE MEXICAN FOOD FART

This fart most commonly occurs after a dog nibbles an enchilada or something that has fallen to the ground outside a Taco Bell. The hot Mexican spices are foreign to a dog's gastrointestinal system and set up such a tumult in the dog's middle, that a fart is produced that can set dry grass on fire. The fart is one of the main reasons fast food aficionados carry fire extinguishers in their cars.

THE CHEWING ON PIECES OF WOOD ALL DAY WHAT-DO-YOU EXPECT FART

A fart of the younger dog. Older dogs are smart enough not to chew on dirty old pieces of wood all day, filling themselves up with cellulose that not only doesn't taste very good, but makes you gassy. This fart comes out with a whoosh whoosh sound but it doesn't smell bad at all.

THE CAR CHASER FART

This is a little known fart due to the fact that most car chasing takes place outdoors and dog farts, like the human variety, are easy to tolerate in the wide open spaces. The fart occurs as the dog is sprinting after the car, as if to provide a little rocket assistance at the critical moment to enable the animal to snatch a tire in its powerful jaws. It's just as well that this boost doesn't work and usually no one, least of all the people in the car, notice it occurred at all.

THE SOILING FART

Even carefully house broken dogs occasionally have an accident. If the dog is also endowed with above average intelligence, he or she may try to put the discovery of the error off a bit by misleading you with a Soiling Fart. Done strictly to buy time, the dog draws you away from the mess that has been made and hopes you won't find it. This gambit never works, but conscience-stricken dogs keep trying.

THE LIVING ROOM FART

This fart is similar to the TV Fart except the numbing distraction of a TV is missing, so the dog is a bit more alert. Your pet understands that living room conversation is not often about dogs and feels a bit left out. A dog will often fart just to draw a little attention to itself, even when it realizes the fart is likely to prompt his or her removal. If just family members are sitting around, this fart is often handled like the TV Fart. In fact, however, people seldom sit in a living room with their own family. The living room is for company, which leads us to the Dreaded Company Fart.

THE DREADED COMPANY FART

Everyone is familiar with this fart. It's the dog fart sure to get the poor pet tossed out of the house. The entire group is embarrassed, as can be expected, and some hostesses keep a can of air freshener by the couch for this emergency. As often as not, of course, the farter is one of the guests who thinks he's gotten away with something by the semi-clever ploy of farting and then looking quizzically at the dog. The dog is never fooled.

THE CARROT FART

Dogs that hang around horses see people giving carrots to horses and figure it's something good 'cause anything dogs see anyone else eat, they think is good for them and might as well go into their stomachs also. So these dogs eat carrots, but since doggy digestive systems just aren't designed for carrots, they fart something awful. It's a vegetable fart which is more pungent than putrid. They also poop orange poop.

THE EATING THE WRONG SIZE DOG BISCUIT FART

Dog biscuits come in small, medium and large sizes and woe to the owner who feeds his or her pet the wrong size. Too small or too big a biscuit will cause the dreaded Dog Biscuit Fart which not only stinks up the room but reoccurs with disturbing frequency until the box is all used up.

THE DINING ROOM FART

This is the classic of all dog farts and surely an entire book could be devoted to its various forms. Dogs will never miss an opportunity to join the family in a dining room. Someone always drops something or can be prevailed upon for a scrap or two. In between, the dog can lie comfy under the table watching everyone's shoes. It's a scene of contentment and happiness to any canine, and a contented dog is a dog that can't restrain a little fart.

THE DINING ROOM FART

Once your pet has reminded everyone of his or her presence with a small emission, banishment usually follows quickly. The one exception is when a new dish is being served and no one can be sure if the aroma is from the food or the dog. Really clever animals get away with murder when new odors saturate a dining room.

THE ROLL-OVER FART

If you're going to ask man's best friend to do dumb, humiliating tricks like rolling over and playing dead, you deserve to get hit with the resulting fart which, if you're not careful, will hit you square in the face. The unpleasantness of this fart depends mainly on yesterday's diet, but the responsibility is always the master's.

THE DRYING OFF FART

You know how dogs shake to dry themselves. Well, as often as not, they shake loose a fart when they do this, but you are so busy dodging the water spray that I bet you've never even noticed it.

THE SLEEPING DOG FART

More dogs have been to veterinary psychologists because of this fart than for any other reason. The poor animal is awakened from a nap by a human yelling and sending the bewildered dog away, and the confused animal has no idea what's happened. The dog probably would have no idea what happened, even if he'd been awake.

THE FORMAL COMPANY FART

As previously discussed, with regular type company you just tell the dog to leave the room and maybe spray a little air freshener around. Formal company is different—these are people you are trying to impress, you know, clergymen, future in-laws, bosses—and in this kind of setting no one's going to bring up the subject of a dog's farting. What happens is really a scream. Man's best friend cuts a little fart. Everyone sits around looking at each other wondering what to do and feeling more and more uncomfortable as the odor permeates the clothes and very pores of the guests and host alike. At times like this, a great leader is required who will call the group to dinner or suggest everyone retire to the porch. Tell Fido to stay when you leave the room.

THE SNAPPING AT BUGS FART

You probably don't imagine that snapping at and even catching a few bugs would cause farting in a dog, but medical science has proven otherwise. It seems your dog swallows lots of air in this activity and air has to come out somewhere, or your poor pooch would blow up like a balloon. Fortunately, the Snapping At Bugs Fart is mostly just air and it hardly offends at all.

THE CONFINED SPACE RULE

Given a choice of farting in a confined space, say a closed car, a dog will always choose that, rather than, perhaps, a giant 4-car garage. If you are working in a closet or cramped space in the attic, the dog will always prefer to fart there rather than in a living room or hallway.

THE ROAD KILL FART (FRESH)

Fresh road kill doesn't necessarily generate worse farts than the normal meat a dog eats. It's the fur and feathers you have to watch out for. These have a habit of reappearing at inappropriate times, often in a gaseous state, and the smell will be so unusual that you won't at first know where it's coming from. You might find yourself saying, "Honey, are you burning chicken feathers in the kitchen?" or, "Is the cat in the microwave again?"

THE ROAD KILL
FART
(RIPENED)

Never, never let a dog into the house after they have eaten some ripened road kill. Your beloved pet will surely do something terrible on your favorite carpet, but the farts—and this can last for two days, will make your house uninhabitable. A good stout rope—better yet, a chain and a spot in the garage—is the solution to this irresistible dining sensation.

THE DREADED VET FART

Somehow dogs always seem to know when you are taking them to the vet and if your dog is like most, this is not one of his favorite trips. The dog gets nervous as the car makes the familiar turns and the poor animal becomes so agitated as you get closer, that farting is a forgone conclusion. And what farts they are! These are called "dreaded" for a very good reason and this trip is definitely one of the open windows variety.

When you get to the vet it's a good opportunity to ask the doctor about controlling your pet's gas problem. The vet doesn't have an idea how to do this anymore than you do but since he or she is a doctor, will mumble something about feeding your dog less and cutting out between meal snacks and people foods. It's a rare dog that will actually fart in the vet's office, so the vet really doesn't have much experience with the problem.

THE VET FART

THE TURKEY BONE FART

Dogs not lucky enough to get the turkey leftovers sometimes have success in the garbage can with the turkey carcass. Don't believe that old myth about chicken and turkey bones causing dogs to choke. Dogs are much too smart to choke on something that tastes so good. The real problem with a whole turkey carcass is that all those soft bones are going to trap a lot of air in your dog's insides and the resultant farts are among the bulkier blasts. The Turkey Bone Fart is one of the few that is almost always noisy and often wakes a sleeping dog with quite a start.

THE BEDROOM FART

People who invite their dogs to share their bedrooms have only themselves to blame when they are awakened, often choking in the middle of the night, by the Bedroom Fart. The poor dog who has been fast asleep hasn't the slightest idea of why he or she is being ejected so suddenly from a comfy deep sleep. More emotionally unstable dogs can blame their behavior problems on the Bedroom Fart than on any other factor.

THE FLEA FART

Your itching dog rolls to one side and gets some vigorous scratching going. The change of position loosens a small fart. That's all there is to it. What's the big deal? For all you know, the smell dislodges a few fleas as well.

THE GREEN FOG BULLDOG FART

Do bulldogs fart more than other dogs? Trish, a lady from Eastern Massachusetts, writes that her bulldog, Gus, farts loud, noisy farts so thick, they leave a green fog. When guests come over, she's too embarrassed to let them into rooms at the back of the house where Gus hangs out. Most people have never heard a noisy dog fart, but this information seems to prove otherwise. You don't want to hear the story about the day Gus ate three pounds of dry cat food and blew up like a balloon.

THE BUTT DRAGGING SYNDROME

This isn't really a fart but more an especially disgusting habit. Dogs will sometimes drag their butt along your best carpet. They have an unnerving preference for the most expensive oriental or wall-to-wall in your house for this particular trick. No one knows if it's an itch or just revenge for your keeping most of the really good snacks for yourself.

THE TERRITORIAL FART

Some dogs pee to establish the boundaries of their territory but within a house, where this act is vigorously frowned upon, a dog can use farts. This is especially true in a house full of pets where multiple dogs and cats and God knows what else compete for space and attention. The owners of dogs that use the Territorial Fart tend to have very low thresholds of smell.

THE CHEWED UP RUBBER BALL FART

Common as fire hydrants. Coco works on an old rubber ball for a few hours of fun in the afternoon and after diligently chewing it to death, manages to swallow a few pieces. It doesn't taste good enough to finish, but the damage is done and a sort of melted rubber smell is going to be noticed before the evening is over.

THE SNORING FART

Lots of dogs snore and people sometimes think the noise, especially when it comes out all of a sudden as a kind of snort, is a fart. It's not at all. There really is no such thing as a snoring fart. More dogs have been made compulsive by being awakened from a sound and innocent sleep with their masters screaming at them to get the hell out of the room, than any other reason.

THE PROUD AS PUNCH FART

This is an announcement fart, a proud fart, when the dog knows it has done a good job. Common among hunting dogs, the animal comes to your feet wagging its tail vigorously, expecting its praise, but in the exuberance of the moment lets slip a dandy fart. The master recoils and yells, and the dog can't figure out what he or she did wrong. If it weren't for the fact that dogs have such short memories, they'd all be neurotic.

THE STOCKY DOG* FART

*St. Bernards, Mastiffs, Newfoundlands, Rottweilers

Stocky dogs have the weight and build to lay a fart that has some real substance and volume. Because of the size and strength of these dogs, they cannot be easily banished when they misbehave, and their farts can quickly empty an entire home of humans, as well as any other breathing creatures that have the misfortune to be in the area.

THE CHINESE FOOD FART

Leftover Chinese food is best relegated to the garbage disposal after it's rested a few days in your refrigerator. If you feed it to your dog or the clever fellow finds it in the garbage, you're going to be evacuating rooms a few hours later. The Chinese Food Fart has a horrible stench, but two minutes later it has gone away.

PLEKASAURUS

THE BONE CHEWING FART

Give a dog a bare bone and likely as not the poor thing will chew on it for hours, trying to get only a dog knows what kind of goodness out of it. The scrap of meat is long gone, you can see the marrow has dropped out, but still your pet chews away. A persistent dog will suck on the dry parts till it all but disappears. This calcium, which is what the bone is made of, once deposited in the dog's stomach, leads to the Bone Chewing Fart, which is as natural and ordinary a dog fart as there is.

THE TUG OF WAR FART

This favorite game of all dogs produces a sharp report of a fart, aromatic and lasting. All the muscles of a dog's body are towing and jerking and this fart comes out like a rocket. Some think that dogs can do this fart purposely, just to distract you and win the game, but they are often the same people who claim their dogs think they are people.

THE WRONG AGE DOG FOOD FART

Only a simpleton believes in this fart. The clever marketers who sell dog food categorize the foods by age to enable them to get more shelf space and to sell **you** more dog food. They'll have you believe that feeding one-year-old food to a puppy or mature dog food to a two-year-old will cause this fart. Tell them what you think by buying the generic stuff.

THE FINALLY CAUGHT THE SKUNK FART

This is a fart that nobody ever smells. Old Yeller and Duke are banished to a bucket of tomato juice and are miserable and smelly enough so no one is going to notice a fart or two. The odor passes in a few days and few dogs bother with a skunk a second time.

THE GUESS WHAT I FOUND THIS MORNING IN THE YARD FART

This fart is so truly horrible that you wonder how any animal, no matter how hungry, could have put something in its stomach that was so rank as to evolve into a fart like this. Dad will be glad he has gone to work when this one cuts loose. Should no one be home at the time of this grand discharge, you will note its effects by the dead moths, ants and other insects on the floor when you return.

THE SCOLDING FART

The poor dog farts. The owner scolds and a nervous dog becomes upset and looses another fart. This unfortunate chain reaction is all too common with your more emotionally unstable dogs and often continues till the poor creature has farted every bit of air in its intestinal tract and is constipated for the next two days.

THE MISDEMEANOR FART

Old Fido has just eaten the cheese dip put out for your company or quite accidently peed on the new oriental carpet. Now he is lying low, trying to be as unobtrusive as possible, perhaps even hiding in a favorite closet. Feeling as he does, just calling his name will usually cause him to loose the Misdemeanor Fart, a short but intense fart whose terrible odor explains the turmoil that has been going on in Fido's conscience.

THE READY TO EAT FART

In this happiest moment of a dog's day, it is common for the excitement to overcome doggy, and he'll let a small, almost totally inoffensive fart slip out. This joyful fart seldom bothers anyone.

THE OVERSEXED DOG FART

Some male dogs are just oversexed and when bitches are not available, will mount other male dogs, furniture and people's legs with impunity. Some become so excited that they fart at moments like this, leading to the small and only moderately odorous Oversexed Dog Fart. Understandably, most people object to having their legs mounted by a farting dog no matter how moderate the farts, so these dogs have few friends.

THE ANTIPASTO FART

Sometimes a dog will fart a little fart and then really cut loose with a big one. This little first fart is called the Antipasto Fart and its purpose is to alert everyone so when the big one comes, everyone is riveted on the proud creature. The dog gets sent from the room, of course, just the same.

RIN TIN TIN

THE
SOME DOGS
NEVER FART
FART

The noble dogs of the cinema, in years gone by, never farted—Rin Tin Tin, Old Yeller, Lassie, Benji, Beethoven. Could you possibly imagine these dogs farting? Well, maybe Beethoven. I think Beethoven farted in one movie, but the rest probably never farted in their entire lives.

THE JOGGING ALONG FART

Some breeds are natural lopers and can run all day, and most dogs can out sprint a human over short distances, but few dogs are dumb enough to try to keep up with joggers doing five or ten miles at a time. Since your dog loves you, he or she will run along as long as possible. When you get home and have your shower and beer, your pet will show you what they think of your exercise routine by lying and farting for the rest of the day.

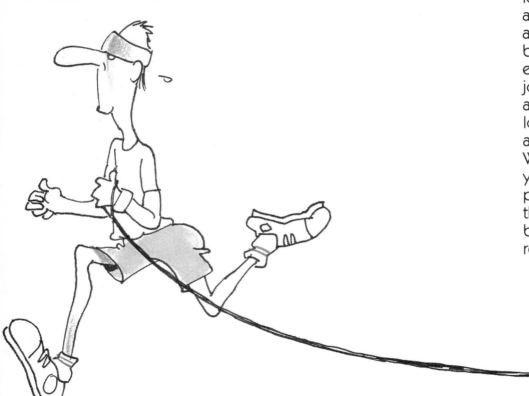

THE TAIL'S REAL FUNCTION

Dog books explain that dogs use their tails to help maintain their balance. Anyone, however, who has owned a dog that tends towards gassiness knows that its real function is to try to dissipate the fart before its master notices and scolds. This plan never works. The tail, as often as not, spreads the fart around bringing it even sooner to an owner's attention. The dog would do better to be still and hope the fart did the same, avoiding the noses of the humans and eventually sinking into the carpet.

THE UP ON THE BED FART

It's bad enough that some people let their dogs sleep in their bedroom, but some fools invite their pets up on the bed with them. Dogs love to sleep on your bed where they are snuggly comfortable and can keep an eye on their masters in case, for example, the master should decide to get up in the middle of the night to get a little something to eat.

1

2

From this commanding position, the dog is well placed to let loose the Up On The Bed Fart which has annoyed owners for years. Fortunately, most people who invite dogs onto their beds don't have all that good a sense of smell in the first place.

THE UP ON THE BED FART

3

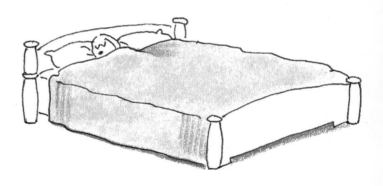

4

THE DOG SCHOOL FART

In obedience schools, the dogs are all kept rigidly controlled with choke chains and a teacher who emphasizes discipline with a firm hand. One dog farts. This sets off a chain reaction of ass sniffing and turmoil that turns the class into a circus. For passersby, it's really quite amusing to watch.

THE GUARD DOG FART

You mix a timid guard dog and a stressful situation and what often results is the Guard Dog Fart. The easily alarmed animal farts, rather than attacking the intruder, but unless it's one hell of a fart, this approach rarely succeeds in deterring the trespassers. Dogs that rely on this technique seldom get the really good-paying guard dog jobs.

THE GARBAGE CAN FART

A traditional source for farts of the phoot, phoot variety. Smelly and lingering, it gives you plenty of incentive to buy a tighter fitting garbage can lid. The exact fragrance of this most common dog fart is totally a function of the quality of the garbage.

The neighbor's garbage is always much more interesting to your dog than your own. A little taste of adventure and the unknown, I suppose. Any dog worth its salt would much rather rummage through someone else's garbage than just a rehash of all the stuff already sampled at their own home. This seeking of variety leads to a wide range of malodorous emissions that defies description.

THE NEIGHBOR'S GARBAGE CAN FART

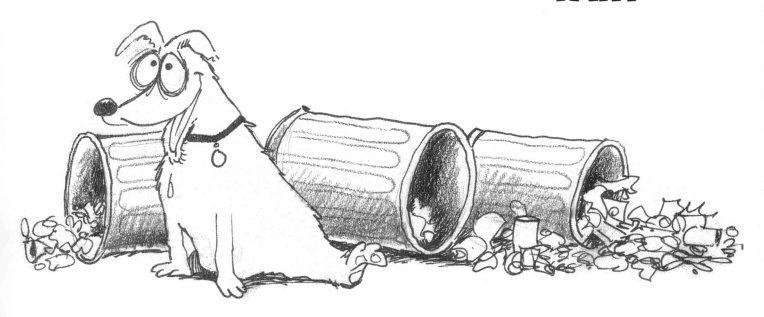

THE VISITING SOMEONE ELSE'S HOUSE FART

As embarrassing as it is to have your dog fart when company is over, it's positively mortifying when your darling does it in someone else's home. The proper etiquette on this occasion is for the dog owner himself (women seldom fart) to pretend he farted, take the blame and ask to use a toilet.

THE CAT DID IT FART

A clever farting dog will often intimate that the cat did it. The dog senses your annoyance over the fart and registers his or her disapproval as well by rising and perhaps sniffing a bit at the cat. It's surprising how often this little trick works.

THE SWIMMER'S FART

This rare dog fart is the only one that can actually be seen. As your pet is furiously paddling, his or her head extended high to keep it out of the water, a fart produces a series of bubbles behind. Most dogs don't even notice, but in calm waters this bubbling can be unsettling to timid animals. It's as though some water monster is following your pet and it encourages this kind of dog to swim with much vigor.

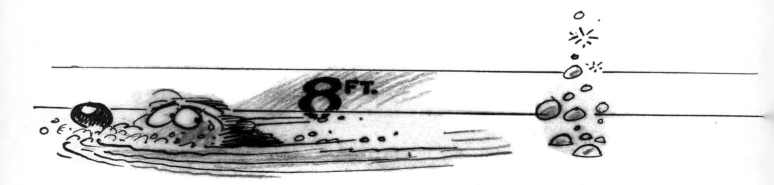

THE JUMPING UP AND DOWN FART

Teasing your dog and getting your pet to jump up for some treat for fifteen minutes might be fun and good exercise for the animal, but you'll pay for it later when all the stuff in his or her middle, having been jumbled together, generates the enormous Jumping Up And Down Fart. This is one of the canine family's rare noisy farts, and comes about thirty minutes after the game is over.

THE FATTY DUCK FART

Once a neighbor's dog got into the garbage and found the remains of several fatty duck dinners. The poor fellow ate so much he almost died, but in the process farted some truly remarkable farts, bursting and loud, much like a cacophony of quacks. This is the only occurrence, as far as I know, of this fart but for completeness' sake, I wanted to include it.

THE DOG HOUSE FART

This is another fart myth. People may build dogs dog houses, but dogs never go into them unless bribed. It's doubtful they ever fart in dog houses, but then again how would you know?

THE DROPPED ON THE FLOOR ICE CREAM FART

Dogs are not fed ice cream on a regular basis, but when some falls on the ground, they are usually first on the scene. Perhaps their digestive systems aren't made for milk products, certainly some dogs have an inability to handle lactose, but whatever the reason, the ice cream fart is a killer that has the potential of putting Häagen Dazs **and** Ben & Jerry's out of business.

THE DRINKING OUT OF THE TOILET BOWL FART

A bad one that I can hardly write about in a book meant for family consumption. Forget to put the lid down on a toilet and doggy is going to use it for a water fountain no matter how full and clean his regular bowl. You'll yell and your dog will feel guilty and he or she will fart and that's all there is to it.

THE LEFTOVER PIZZA FART

Better to waste the food. People in China really aren't starving these days. Feed a leftover pizza to your dog and you'd better hope it's summertime 'cause one of you is going to be spending a lot of time outdoors. The Pizza Fart is one of the worst smelling dog farts of them all, that usually announces its presence with a kind of shleept, shleept sound. Dogs, incidentally, like pepperoni pizza best.

THE TOY* FART
*Toy Poodles, Maltese, Pekingese, Pomeranian, Yorkshire Terrier

A little foosh sound can sometimes be heard, or at least that's the sound you'd imagine for a fart that is so tiny as to hardly have a noticeable odor. You have to be pretty close to your pet to even realize the Toy Fart has occurred.

THE BEER FART

Never, ever teach your dog to drink beer. It'll make them fart all day, not to mention bugging you to go outside to pee. Dogs don't naturally like beer and the jackasses who teach them to drink it deserve all the grief they get.

THE KENNEL FART

Out of sight, out of mind. People go through entire lives of dog ownership without even knowing this fart exists. What do you expect? Your poor pet is locked up in a strange place with strange people, food and smells and lots of other scared dogs and you'd better believe he or she is going to fart like all hell. Most kennel owners have totally lost their sense of smell, much like teenagers lose hearing from turning up their walkmen too loud.

THE SUNDAY FART

You wouldn't think dogs know one day of the week from another, especially not with respect to their farting activity, but there you are—the whole family relaxed amidst sports pages and comics and guess who comes out with the smelliest fart of the week. It is unexplainable, but aptly named the Sunday Fart.

THE WORKING DOG FART

By definition, these are out-of-doors serious dogs often holding down more than one full-time job, and their farts are working class farts. When employed with duties, however, that require stealth and scenting skills, excessive farting can seriously affect job performance, and working dogs that have a tendency toward flatulence are often the first you see in unemployment lines.

THE YANK YOUR OWNER AFTER A RODENT FART

Very similar to the Tug Of War Fart and since it usually occurs outdoors, this fart has been ignored for years. Many owners, concentrating on maintaining their balance or keeping the straining animal from yanking their shoulder from its socket, do not even notice it and very little study has been done on its characteristics.

THE TWINKIE FART

Dogs shouldn't eat junk food and this fart is designed to make you painfully aware of that fact. The Twinkie Fart has a stench more than a mere smell, almost a sticky-sweet foulness that will make you want to drive the dog from the room. Obviously it is too late for that and wise owners take themselves for a walk when this fart occurs and swear never to let their pet near junk food again.

THE AFTER DINNER FART

It doesn't matter if his dog food is dry or wet or even last week's leftover sirloin. Dinner time is like lighting a fuse in your dog's digestive system and the chances are the After Dinner Fart is going to be the result. This fart is a satisfying part of every dog's evening meal and should not be scorned too harshly.

THE POTATO FART

This fart is about as different from a Twinkie Fart as you can get. It takes a hungry or very painstakingly trained dog to eat a potato. Potatoes are not so great for dogs' stomachs, but the resulting fart usually has an earthy flavor not unlike the springtime aroma of slightly rotting hay. The bowel movements that often accompany the Potato Fart are another matter entirely, and you'll be happier if they take place on someone else's lawn.